Wake Up

poems by

Joyce Sweeney

Finishing Line Press
Georgetown, Kentucky

Wake Up

Copyright © 2017 by Joyce Sweeney
ISBN 978-1-63534-155-3 First Edition
All rights reserved under International and Pan-American Copyright Conventions.
No part of this book may be reproduced in any manner whatsoever without written permission from the publisher, except in the case of brief quotations embodied in critical articles and reviews.

ACKNOWLEDGMENTS

These poems first appeared in the following journals:

Broken Bridge: Being a Poet Is Harder Than I Remembered
Meridian Anthology of Contemporary Poetry: Gatekeeper
the Kerf: Eve Fallen
Rockhurst Review: Princess
Earth's Daughters: Tectonics

Publisher: Leah Maines

Editor: Christen Kincaid

Cover Art: Joyce Sweeney

Author Photo: Jay Sweeney

Cover Design: Elizabeth Maines McCleavy

Printed in the USA on acid-free paper.
Order online: www.finishinglinepress.com
          also available on amazon.com

Author inquiries and mail orders:
Finishing Line Press
P. O. Box 1626
Georgetown, Kentucky 40324
U. S. A.

Table of Contents

Being a Poet Is Harder Than I Remembered 1
Gatekeeper 2
Jeffrey 3
Eve Fallen 4
Carousel Waltz 5
Night Rain 6
Definitive Journey 7
Losing Altitude 8
Answered Prayer 9
Twister 10
Helpless 11
Broken Cocoon 12
Dual Diagnosis 13
Her Room 14
Withdrawal 15
3 AM 16
Cloudburst 17
Shedding 18
In the Eye 19
The Dying Thing 20
Princess 21
Recovering 22
Ribbon Snake 23
Tectonics 24
Then You Walk On and Forget 25

To Irene Mary
1957 – 2011

Being a Poet Is Harder Than I Remembered

I had forgotten how the room and everyone in it
disappears into a gold fog
when an idea descends
My soundtrack changed from Matt Lauer to Keiko Matsui
morning walk disturbed by sudden chains of words I fear I'll forget

I had no idea, the disruption, the chaos I would unleash
Spiral notebook morphing into this bound journal with birds on it,
Endless drafts, piles of paper on the floor
the dove release of emails and envelopes
I miss meals, don't plan my outfits so well

And sometimes my feet tilt off the ground a little

Fiction is a masked dance with proscribed steps
Poetry is a windstorm that blows the room apart
forcing unlikely things to collide

My mask is shattered
I can no longer hide my anger
I'm exhausted, reduced to elements,
stripped, breathless
in love

Gatekeeper

My front door is double and hollow
lovingly refinished every year
glossy as ganache
A tiny gap at the top
allows hurricane-force winds and very tiny lizards to get through
The left side droops; my students have to pull hard to come in for class
This is the first lesson in writing: you have to pull hard on the door

On our side, we get ready for Thanksgiving
My refugee cat watches me chop celery
Tail tip flicks as he tastes stock simmering in the air
On the other side, broken duck eggs
from the nest Josephine built in August
Napoleon's youngest wife, the clear favorite
She hasn't had a good nest yet, raccoons find them all
But she and I have hope for next summer
A spider weaves diagonals across the front of the door like Miss America sashes
Every time I go out for the mail, I break them
Every time, she reweaves

Beyond that, a shimmery morning breeze, a stand of queen palms
the people across the street who hide a Christmas tricycle in their garage
an overcast sky and infinity

Jeffrey

Seconds after you die, we hear the crash
Foundations shake, birdfeeder bucks
In a haze of burning grass and melting steel, we see your Infiniti
spun backwards in our yard, five feet from the kitchen window
We call 911—the police drench us in light
Far from the car, they find you—a white cloth flutters down
They cover what they cannot save
Lights sweep the backyard, searching for others
but you were alone
Next morning, yellow tape and photographs
They miss your shoes, your cell phone
When the tow lift pulls, your Infiniti shatters
Later, we venture out, walk the path of your riderless car
look for clues—your beer bottle, the program from the concert
An officer comes back for the shoes and phone, tells us we can pick up the rest ourselves
I stuff cupholders and wiper blades into a trash bag, attracting neighbors like a celebrity
Someone says the police ID'd you—you were one week from your 21st birthday
celebrating early
If I had children, my sons would be your age
I watch the papers faithfully for the one piece of the story no one tells me
Your first name

Eve Fallen

I clean in an orgiastic frenzy
like my mother; shaking out snowy linens,
inhaling caustic cleansers, spinning plates under streams of
cold water
When it's done, I look out the kitchen window
to see a thin, green snake
threading the grass, like a live river
Pausing, he lifts his head, licks the air, then looks straight at me

Most of my friends hate housework, pay to have it done
freeing them to catch up on news, read books, surf the net
None of those word games are as real to me as the dust on the surface of
things,
the slow dance of objects around a room

While the snake looks at me and I at him
we are both completely alive
Then the phone rings—I turn away and he's gone,
quick as a blessing
leaving me with another friend who wants to pour words in my ear

Carousel Waltz

Swamped by fevers and delirious drugs
I answer the same email three times
and
give
up
What a relief!

To be a child, wrapped in an old sweater
people worrying and thinking about me
savoring the guilty pleasure of reality shows
where strangers dance, cook, sew
and cry over the slightest thing

Like me, later in the day
finding a favorite old movie, *Carousel*
struck, this time, by the thought that my father, whom I try so hard not to think about
might have been looking down on me all these fifty years
crying out, "Somebody ought to help her!"

Night Rain

Day thoughts smolder
Dream fragments skitter across the mind moon
and the night rain spills quiet music
like the sound of a long-lost parent in another room
locking doors, taking care of things

The night rain is my father
His whispers quell the last threads of consciousness
He pours comfort over the roof and down the windows in streams

Making a soft, lapping lake beneath my house
where I can drift back into his arms

Definitive Journey

In this dream, I crouch on the basement steps
With stiff, tense fingers, probe the linoleum's grooved edge
A voice echoes from a loudspeaker—"This is your definitive journey."

Then, a slow grinding,
house foundations splinter and snap
cracking and breaking,
pulling from a dock into open water
I am thrilled to be finally at sea!
My feet pound the stairs, searching for an upper deck
Where I can feel the wind and wake

But above there is no sky—just a beamed attic ceiling,
the rafters drip with dangles of snakes
racers, coaches, vines and whips
I glide beneath them, as they boil, wriggle and twist
inches from my face

Losing Altitude

Mid-July, pressure drops
Everglades rumble under swollen clouds
I lie in limbo between hot flashes
pickled in *pinot grigio*, starving
to carve the post-grief pounds

Outside, spiders hang like dead marionettes
Lizards rock and gasp as my neighbor listlessly shoots off leftover fireworks
The mail truck rolls up—nothing
I turn off the TV to stop the war, close my eyes and pray
for a hurricane to sweep it all clean

Answered Prayer

Hurricane Dean pinwheels the Caribbean
toward Chetumal, where he was once worshipped as the god of change
Safely out of his path, I enjoy the rich bank of chartreuse clouds
stippling the dawn with seeps and sips of margarita light

Sinking air rattles cypress heads like laughter, tints
the formerly glaring sky a sweet forgiving blue
Negative ions purge and purify my scarred lungs
I clean a closet, trashbagging memories that have pinned
me down too long

In a few days, Mexico will be hit, but everything is balanced
Huracan is the only god who seems to hear my prayers
His violent side stream has saved me
from the relentless pressure of being alive

Twister

Dorothy, I know what it's like
to see your house picked up and thrown
with you in it

holding your little pet, crouching on the bed
with your whole life flying
by the window

the car that crashed in your back yard
your first book of poems
your beautiful double door in splinters
unhatched duck eggs scattered

and now that witch, that witch
laughing at you
and you not knowing where anything will land
or if you'll see home again

Helpless

I don't know how to pray for her
Rage warps my good intentions
I have to stop myself
or I'll release doves with poisoned fangs

I don't know how to ignore her
She is wounded and in front of me
I think I saw her before I met her
in the cold, full, burning, screaming moon

Maybe once I was her
Or someday she will be me

Broken Cocoon

Now comes the war in her
 she flew to the point of exhaustion
wings beating like a heart attack
picked up by a hurricane and dropped here
where she lies breathless, on a strange bed
gulping the pure, thin air, deciding which half is going to win

The moth, who flicks lighters under a harsh moon
who chews pills meant to be swallowed
who piles up mattresses in a corner
and shrieks her pain into the mouthpiece of a dead phone

or the butterfly she always saw in the distance
its velvety, sun-hot wings zooming into the heart of a summer flower

Dual Diagnosis

Maybe she will start a glass of chocolate milk in the pink glass but decide she really wants Coke in the green glass but the chocolate milk is already started and she will be crouched in the corner, finding a bug to keep in a jar and she goes out the wrong door and leaves it open so anything, even life, might get in, and me, running behind her; picking up, latching, closing, locking, trying to contain her as I contain myself because if she leaves a pin on the floor, surely it will stab someone...Who is really crazy? She who surfs the silken rolls of the river; joyful, sad, furious and then a nap? Or me, watching the clock, organizing all the minutes that flow to my death?

Her Room

She has sliced
up my book of pressed
flowers and pinned
blossoms to the lace tablecloth she stole
from the linen closet to hide
her scars in the mirror that hangs
across from her bed

Withdrawal

Will there really come a day
when I no longer feel her claws sunk into my belly
her fangs pressed to my throat?

Will I sleep without the recurring nightmare of total darkness
her voice hissing threats in my ear?

Outside the window, sun sparkles in street puddles
I remember happiness

But I have been her slave so long
I can't imagine any me separate from her

Yet

3 AM

Between worlds
chartreuse light pools in the black corners of her room
like webs
as she talks, and spins her world

The chartreuse light is inside her
leaking out from her bladed cuts
the brightest, a cross shape near her ankle

She dissects worms, grinds pills, examines scraps of lint
With her glass eye
I gulp water, watch for shifts of light and color
plead silently with the angels, always the same prayer

Stop the spinning, stop the talking, stop the little cuts
set the worms free, let the webs of light unravel
let them
ascend to the sun in fine clouds of dust

Cloudburst

Another spring, the earth swells and sags
bloated with warm rain
simmering under the young sun

Everything ripens in its husk
then thrusts forward

Tiny razor beaks stab fragile shells
Butterflies thrash in soggy cocoons
Kids jam the accelerator and spin out

Flowers burst from stems
Pollen rains like raging fairy dust
Sirens sing, bullets fly
Snakes pour from the ground

Shedding

First, she feels the compression
a tight, fierce, headache, blindness
Then the suffocation begins
every inch of her skin
constricting; her beating heart,
her growling stomach

She tries to distract herself
with the music of rivers turning
the soft thump of butterflies, tapping their cocoons

Every year this panic returns
She needs the panic, it spurs her to act
crack the membrane that clouds her vision
Then comes the frenzy as she writhes
scrapes herself against any rough thing she can find
until the sloughing is complete

She can't help looking back
to see the corpse of who she was
dry, pale, crumpled behind her
before she slithers forward
raw, bright, vulnerable, exposed

In the Eye

Swirling silk scarf caught in a windstorm
Her soul bursts brilliant then dim, hovers
between song and silence as
both sides call to her,
"Wake up!"

The Dying Thing

My husband brought home a dying thing
bundled in cotton wool, breathing softly
brittle and graceful, like a long-limbed grasshopper
She flew out to the sun porch
dried her sodden wings with smoke and rage

We obsessed over her
watched her stretch and preen, then
close up, motionless on nights
when the air-conditioner whistled like the Angel of Death

only to fan open the next day
with new specs of color, like a kaleidoscope of gems
Sometimes she lit gently in our hands
other times flew in our faces, papery wings cutting our eyes
or clamped her teeth on nothing
biting and biting for hours

We loved the dying thing
gave all we had to help her live
but one day, she beat her wings like fury
broke the screens and flew away
so high, so high

Princess

This is why I love him
Walking the campus after Hurricane Wilma
the wind high, but no longer dangerous
He saw Princess, crouched in a nest of swirling grass
Princess, the smallest of the campus cats
the fragile, emotional one
the one who hated to be confined

He didn't see her wild eyes
All he saw was something small that might need help
Before I could stop him, he reached out to her

She clamped his arm with all four sets of claws
biting and biting and biting
He needed seven rabies shots

Sometimes he calls himself a fool
We wouldn't need angels if everyone was a fool like him
Week after week I sat beside him in the emergency room
I will always sit beside him

Recovering

Last night the rain lashed the house in circles
I woke up empty, beached on cold sheets, no reason to get up
until I thought of the dining room chairs

How Mom recovered them so many times when I was little
How she could change her whole world with fabric or paint
How her husband died, died and still she kept recovering

I've been afraid of this job
My generation doesn't sew
But the seats are thirty years old, like my marriage
and now there's a hole you could put your hand through

So I got up, drank coffee, assembled tools and tried to remember how Mom did it
Pulling out the tired old wood screws that held the frame
prying up hundreds of upholstery tacks—tiny, like thorns
Pulling and prying seemed to wake something up in me

I drew away the old shroud of fabric
Placing and tucking the new cloth, I held my breath
my spine rigid to the point of pain, tapping each tiny, fragile thorn-tack back into place

I had to pound my thumb and forefinger—some skin came off
A few corners were imperfect
and I think the stripes are going the wrong way

But the chairs and me are good for another thirty years

Ribbon Snake

Summer again, a full circle
everything has returned in a different form
a ribbon snake is trapped
inside the screened porch—how did she get in?
We put in new screens after the last storm
But there she is, pounding her head against the fine mesh
desperate and frightened

At first I prop the door open, hoping she'll find her way
But in her fear, she can't sense the freedom inches away
Again and again, she pounds her fragile head
on something that won't give

What would anyone do?
I get the broom, frighten her even more
as I sweep her out the door
and back into her life

Tectonics

Being in control is overrated
See how randomly the earth pushes up stones, like little folded messages
to cross your path on a given day when you could hardly breathe
for trying to picture tomorrow or the next day
and steer everything that might happen

Then you see the stone
You might stumble on it, even fall
It wasn't there yesterday

You might pick it up, feel the weight and smoothness
smell the minerals, read the story on its surface where water dripped
where a leaf pressed for several million years
You might put it back and watch it for several days, several walks
One day, darkened by rain, another day sparkling in the sun

Notice how calmly it sits, silent and accepting
until some event, that neither you nor the stone foresaw
takes it somewhere else

Then You Walk On and Forget

You turn a corner on your morning walk
A cloud crosses the sun and the pavement kindles gold
Gates of the universe open: pouring out legions
angels, demons, elves, monsters, lava, poison, snakes,

blood

then you walk on and forget

Joyce Sweeney is the author of fourteen novels for young adults and two chapbooks of poetry. Her first novel, Center Line, won the First Annual Delacorte Press Prize for an Outstanding Young Adult Novel. Many of her books appear on the American Library Association's Best Books List and Quick Picks for Reluctant Readers. Her novel *Shadow* won the Nevada State Reading Award in 1997. Her novel *Players* was chosen by Booklist as a Top Ten Sports Book and by *Working Mother* magazine as a Top Ten for Tweens. Her novel, *Headlock* (Holt 2006), won a Silver Medal in the 2006 Florida Book Awards and was chosen by the American Library Association as a Quick Pick for Reluctant Readers.

Her first chapbook of poems, *IMPERMANENCE*, was published in 2008 by Finishing Line Press.

She has had numerous poems, short stories, articles and interviews published; and her play, *FIRST PAGE CRITIQUES* was produced in 2011.

Joyce has also been a writing teacher and coach for 25 years, beginning with teaching five week classes for the Florida Center for the Book, moving to ongoing invitation only workshops and finally to online classes (www.sweeneywritingcoach.com) which reach students nationally and internationally. Developing strong bonds with the students she critiques and instructs is her hallmark. She believes that writers need emotional support as well as strong, craft-based teaching if they are to make the long, arduous, but very worthwhile journey to traditional publication. At this writing, 57 of Joyce's students have successfully made this journey and obtained traditional publishing contracts.

In 2011, Joyce and a coalition of local playwrights, directors and actors formed The Playgroup LLC, which conducts workshops for playwrights and actors and produces original works by local playwrights. The Playgroup currently presents three productions a year at their home base, The Willow Theatre in Boca Raton.

Joyce lives in Coral Springs with her husband, Jay and caffeine-addicted cat, Nitro.

CPSIA information can be obtained
at www.ICGtesting.com
Printed in the USA
LVOW13s0011240217
525283LV00008B/45/P

9 781635 341553